KNOWING NUMBERS

ACTIVITY BOOK FOR CHILDREN

Count the things in each set and circle the correct number.

a.

4 7 2

b.

3 8 4

What comes before and after?

15

19

9

5 apples and 2 apples is equal to 7 apples

  =

Count and write the numbers.

a.

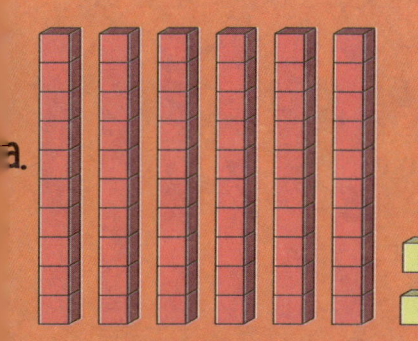

Tens	Ones

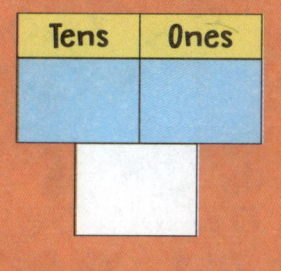

b.

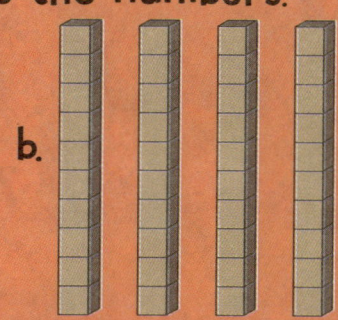

Tens	Ones

Wonder House

What's Missing?

Help the butterfly reach the last flower by filling in the missing numbers.

Color the caterpillar as you write the missing numbers.

a. 1 □ 3 □

b. □ 7 □ 9

c. 4 □ □ 7

d. □ 6 7 □

Let's Count

Match the same number of objects.

a.

b.

c.

d.

1.

2.

3.

4.

Count the things in each set and circle the correct number.

a.

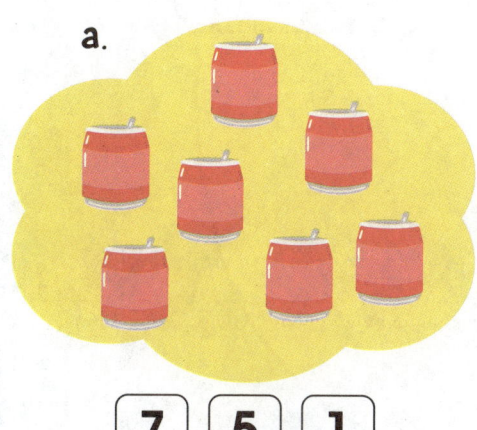

7   5   1

b.

6   2   4

c.

2   1   3

3

Time to Color

Count and write the number of petals of each flower.

a.

b.

c.

d.

Color the picture according to the number key.

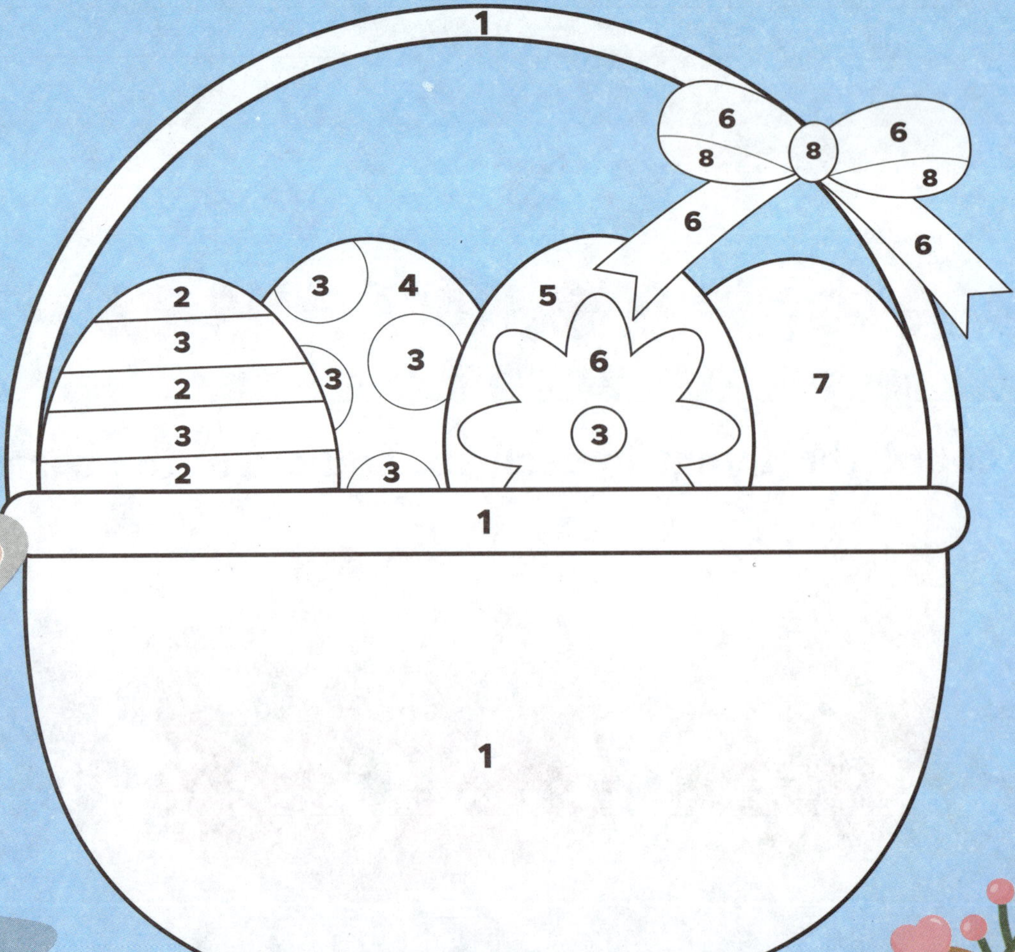

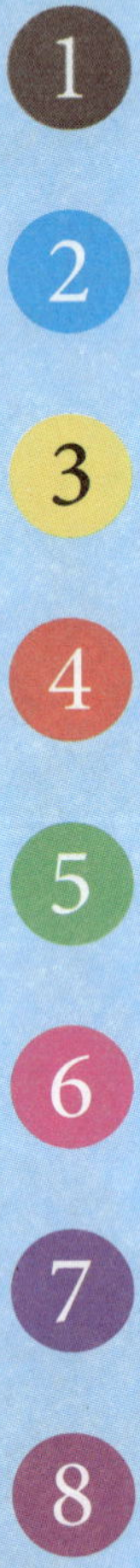

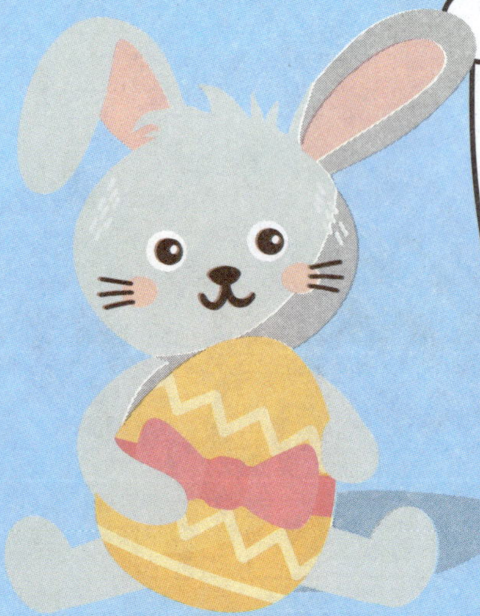

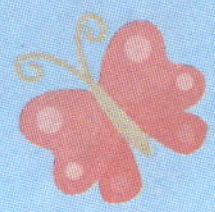

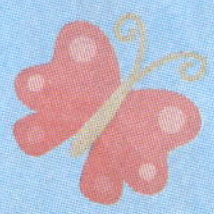

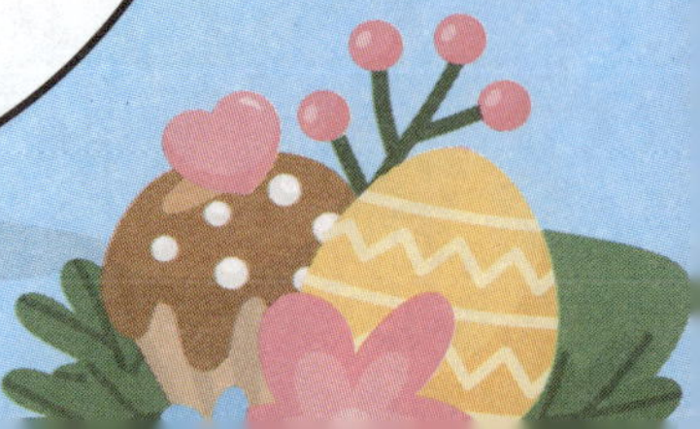

1

6 8 8 6

6 6

2 3 4 5

3 3 6

2 3 7

3 3

2 3

1

1

1
2
3
4
5
6
7
8

Count and Draw

Count the number of things in the right box and draw an equal number of things in the Left box.

a.

balloons

b.

coins

c.

oranges

d.

Leaves

Putting Together

Count and draw the number of dots.

a.

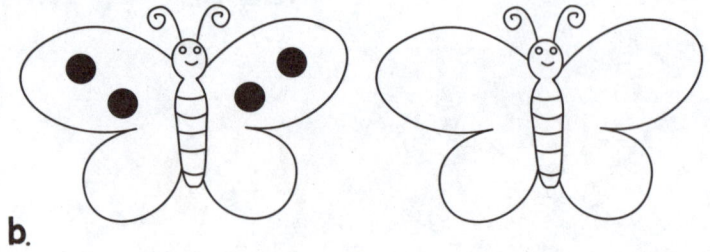

b.

c.

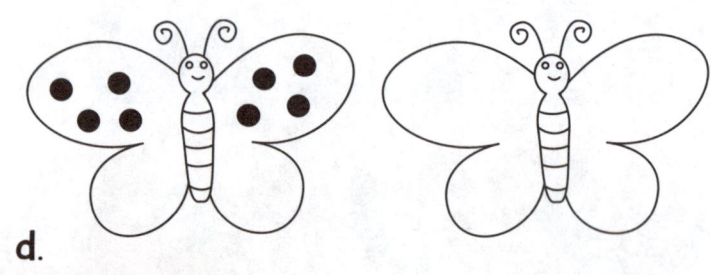

d.

How many altogether?

5 apples and 3 apples is equal to .... apples.

a.

  =

4 cupcakes and 3 cupcakes is equal to .... cupcakes.

b.

  =

3 pears and 2 pears is equal to .... pears.

c.

   =

Addition

The plus symbol (+) is used to represent the addition of two or more expressions.

Add and write.

a. $5+4=$

b. $6+3=$

c. $2+2=$

d. $3+3=$

Let's Add

Count and add.

a.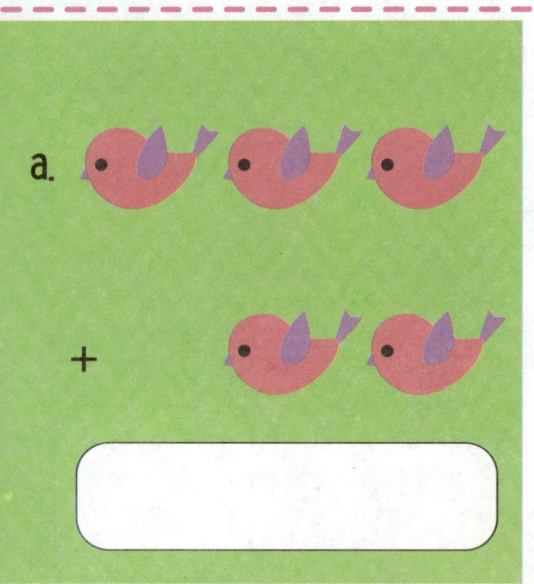

b.

c.

Count the things and match them with their respective equation and answer.

a.

b. (kites)

c. (ladybugs)

d.

4+3

3+2

3+1

5+4

=5

=9

=7

=4

Word Problems

a. You have 3 balloons and your friend has 5 balloons. How many balloons are there altogether?

b. 2 birds were sitting on the fence. 3 more birds came to join them. How many birds are sitting on the fence?

c. You have 5 pieces of candy. Your mom gives you 3 more. How many pieces of candy do you have?

d. Mrs. Hilt made 5 Rice Krispie Treats. She used 2 large marshmallows and 1 mini marshmallow. How many marshmallows did she use altogether?

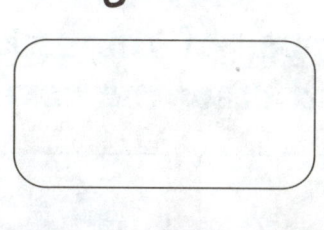

e. There are 6 violins in the store room and 3 violins on display. How many violins are there in total?

f. There are 6 chef assistants and 2 servers. How many staff are working there?

Taking Away

How many are Left?

a.  Take away 2 .... left

b.  Take away 3 .... left

c.  Take away 4 .... left

d.  Take away 1 .... left

Count the number of things in the first box, take away half of it, and draw the remaining in the box below.

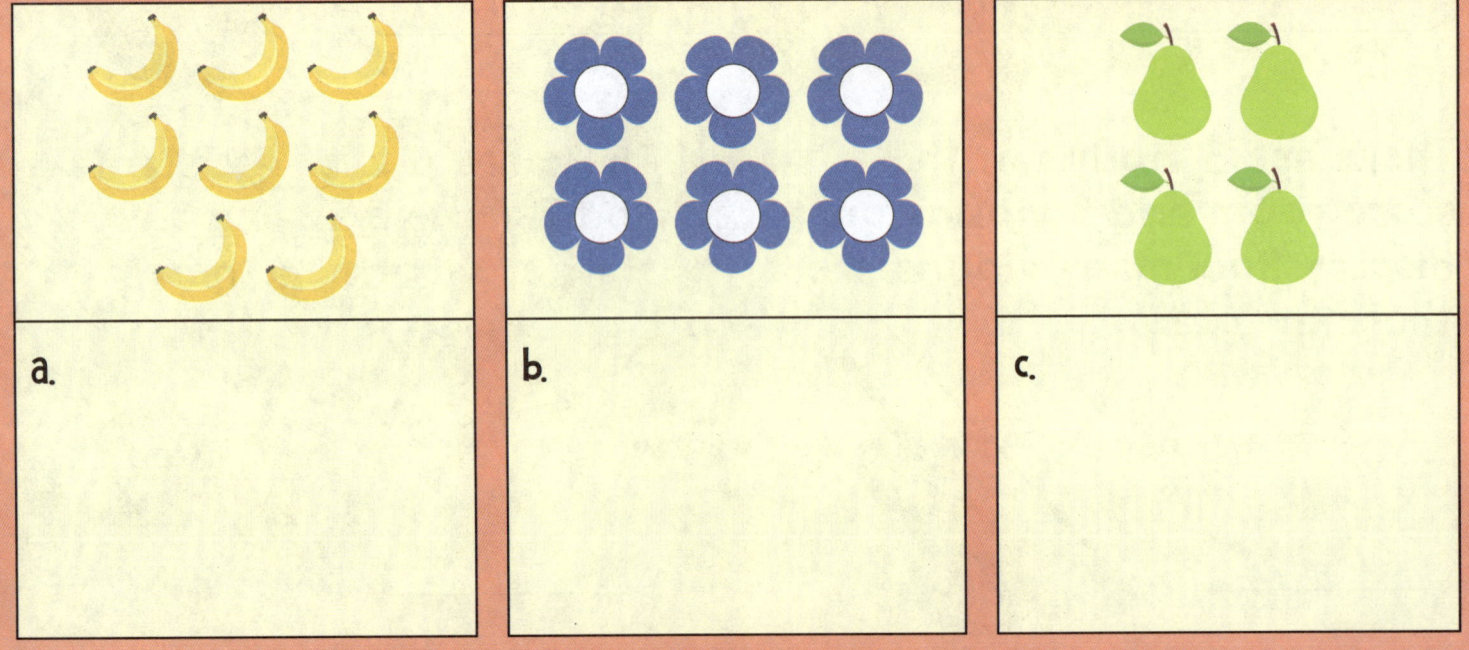

a.

b.

c.

Subtraction

The minus symbol (–) is used to represent the subtraction of two expressions.

Subtract the given numbers by crossing out the objects.

a.  $8-2=$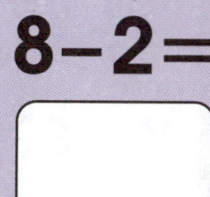

b.  $9-7=$

c.     $5-4=$

d.  $6-3=$

Floral Fun

Solve the problems and color the number of pictures equal to the answer.

a. **8−3=**

b. **7−5=**

c. **4−2=**

Match with the correct answer.

a. **5−4**

b. **7−5**

c. **9−6**

d. **6−2**

1. 4

2. 1

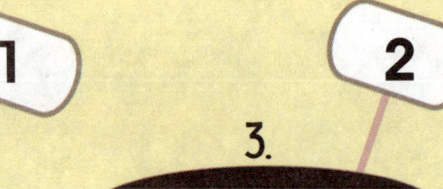

3. 2

4. 3

Wordy Magic

a. Ms. Herold put 5 magazines on the table. Charly, a teacher, took 3 of them and put them back on the shelf. How many magazines were left on the table?

b. There were 8 computers which the students could use for research, but 7 were already occupied. How many computers were still available?

c. Natalia had 6 bags of flour but used up 2 bags on Sunday. How many bags of flour did she have left?

d. Henry packed 9 toy shovels for the beach. 5 took the shovels. How many shovels were left?

e. Dad packed 6 packs of chips to go to the beach and the children ate 5 packs. How many packs of chips are left?

f. Sandy baked 9 boxes of cookies and 3 boxes of muffins. Then she sold 2 boxes of cookies. How many boxes of cookies were left?

Number Line

Draw the jumps on the number line, and write the answer in the box.

a. **5** + **2** = **7**

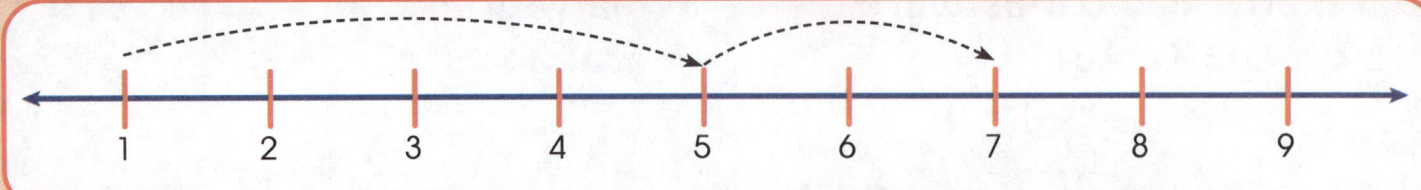

1 2 3 4 5 6 7 8 9

b. **1** + **5** = ◯

1 2 3 4 5 6 7 8 9

c. **3** + **6** = ◯

1 2 3 4 5 6 7 8 9

d. **2** + **6** = ◯

1 2 3 4 5 6 7 8 9

Jump, Add and Subtract

Draw the jumps on the number Line and write the answer in the box.

4+3=

a. [ ]

1 2 3 4 5 6 7 8 9

5+4=

b. [ ]

1 2 3 4 5 6 7 8 9

6+2=

c. [ ]

1 2 3 4 5 6 7 8 9

8+1=

d. [ ]

1 2 3 4 5 6 7 8 9

Draw the jumps on the number Line and write the answer in the box.

a. **6−4=**

1 2 3 4 5 6 7 8 9

b. **9−4=**

1 2 3 4 5 6 7 8 9

Let's Count: Ten to Twenty

Make a group of 10 objects.

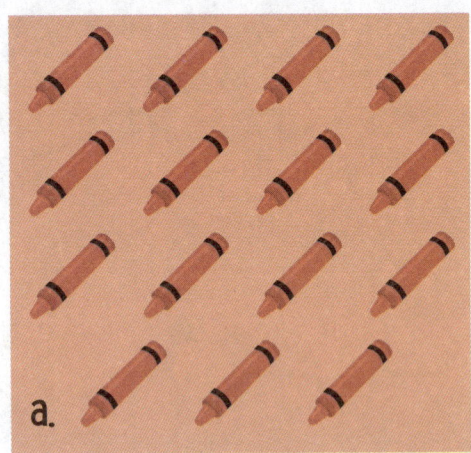

a.

b.

c.

Count and write the number of things in the box.

$10+1=$ ⬜

a.

+

=

$10+6=$ ⬜

b.

+

=

$10+4=$ ⬜

c.

+

=

More or Less?

Color the group with more objects.

a.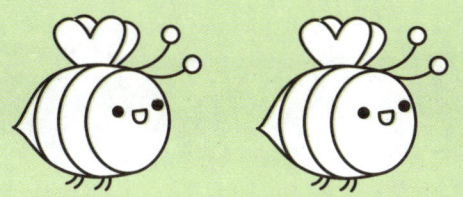

b.

c.

d.

e.

Fill in the missing numbers.

a. 12 ___ 14

b. 13 ___ 15 ___

c. ___ 18 19 ___

Make your way through the maze by following 1–20.

1	8	7	6	7	8
2	3	4	5	6	7
1	2	5	12	11	10	9	8
2	3	4	13	16	16	17	18
7	6	5	14	17	15	18	19
12	7	10	15	18	17	19	20
11	8	9	16	19	20		
10	9	18	17	18	20		

Color the smallest number.

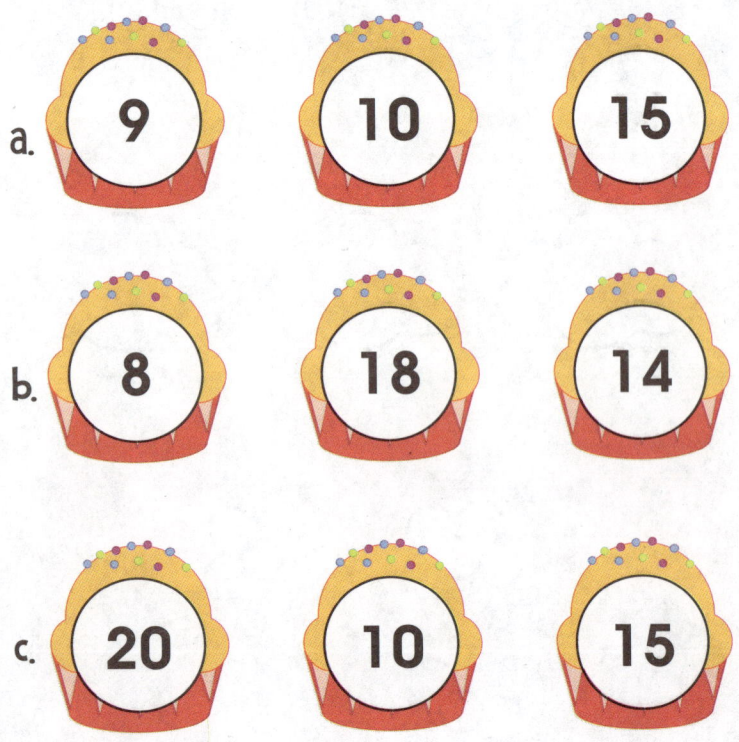

a. 9   10   15

b. 8   18   14

c. 20   10   15

Write the biggest number.

a. 19   b. 6   c. 2

10   17   13

15   2   16

Which Number Am I?

What comes before?

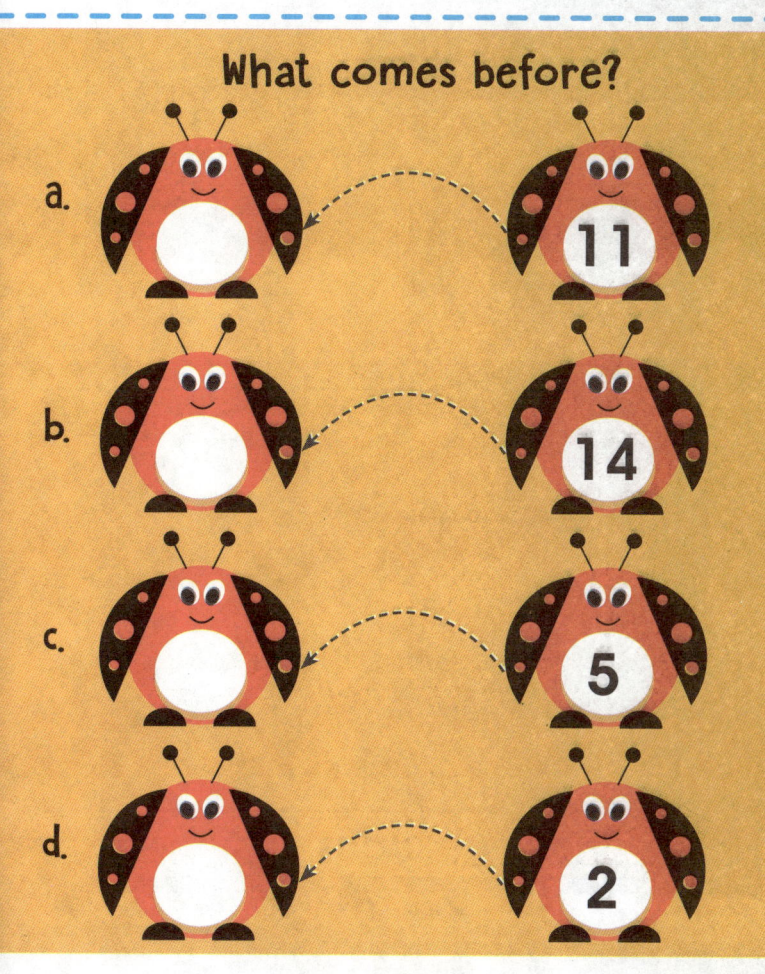

a. 11

b. 14

c. 5

d. 2

What comes after?

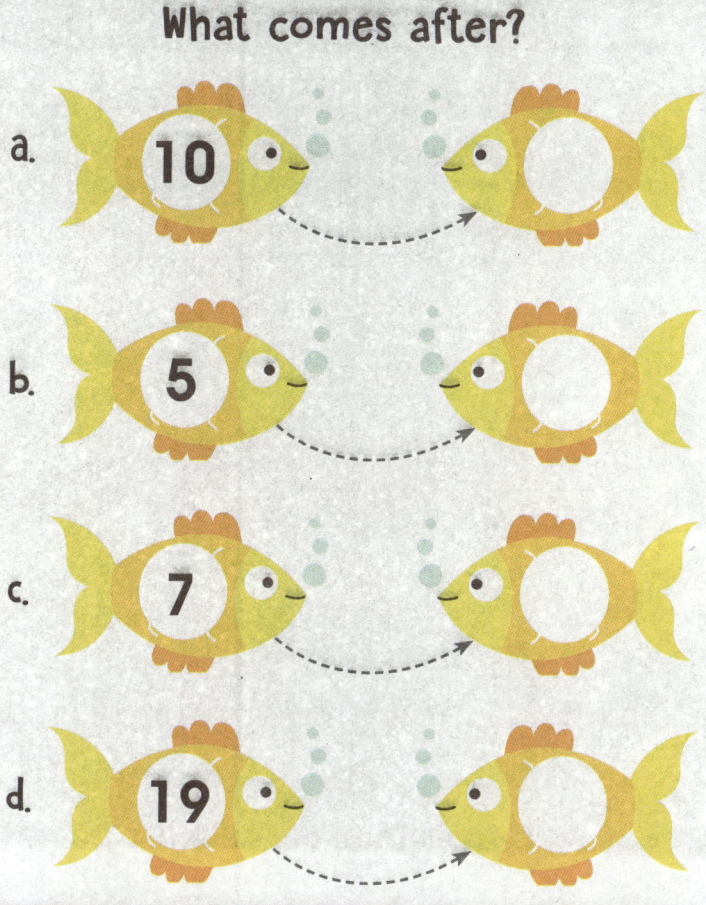

a. 10

b. 5

c. 7

d. 19

What comes in between?

a. 10   12

b. 18   20

c. 4   6

What comes before and after?

a. 15

b. 19

c. 9

Tens and Ones

If a number is made of two digits, we group the number in Tens and Ones to make the counting easier.

Let's take 10 pencils.

Now make a group of 10 pencils.

- We can make only 1 group. It represents 1 Ten. But there is no single pencil remaining. It indicates 0 ones.

- So, the number 10 can be written as:

Tens	Ones
1	0

Count the tens and ones and write them in the boxes.

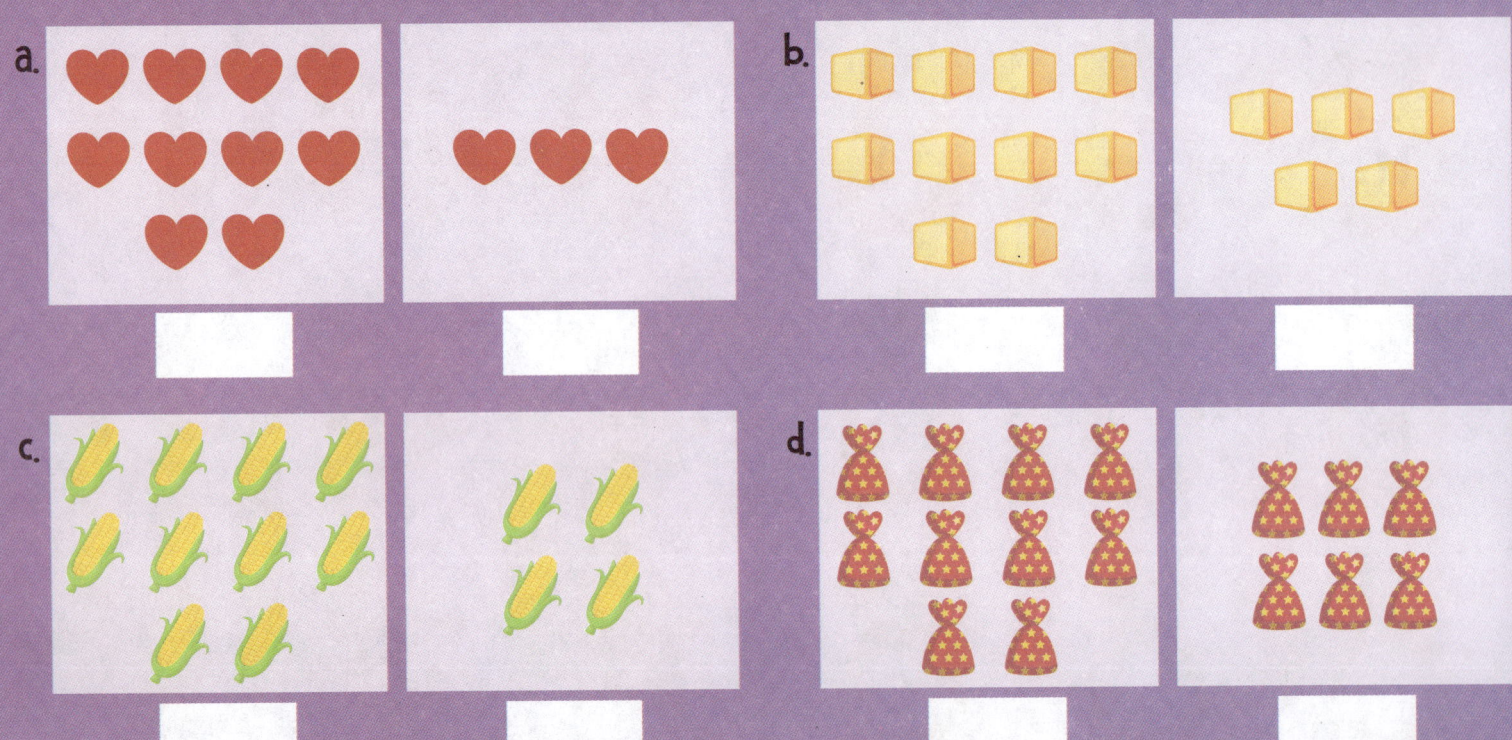

a.

b.

c.

d.

Exploring Tens and Ones

Write how many tens and ones make the number.

a.
20 ....tens and ....ones

b. **14** ....tens and ....ones

c. **12** ....tens and ....ones

d. **18** ....tens and ....ones

Color the correct answer.

a. 1 tens 6 ones
- ○ 18
- ○ 16
- ○ 15

b. 1 tens 3 ones
- ○ 13
- ○ 12
- ○ 10

c. 1 tens 0 ones
- ○ 15
- ○ 10
- ○ 14

d. 2 tens 0 ones
- ○ 17
- ○ 18
- ○ 20

Match the number on the left to the picture on the right.

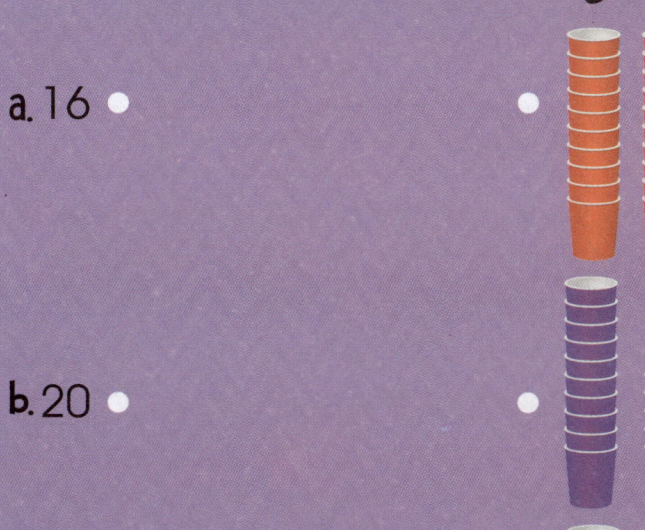

a. 16 •

b. 20 •

c. 15 •

Count the dots in both frames and then add them together. Circle the correct answer.

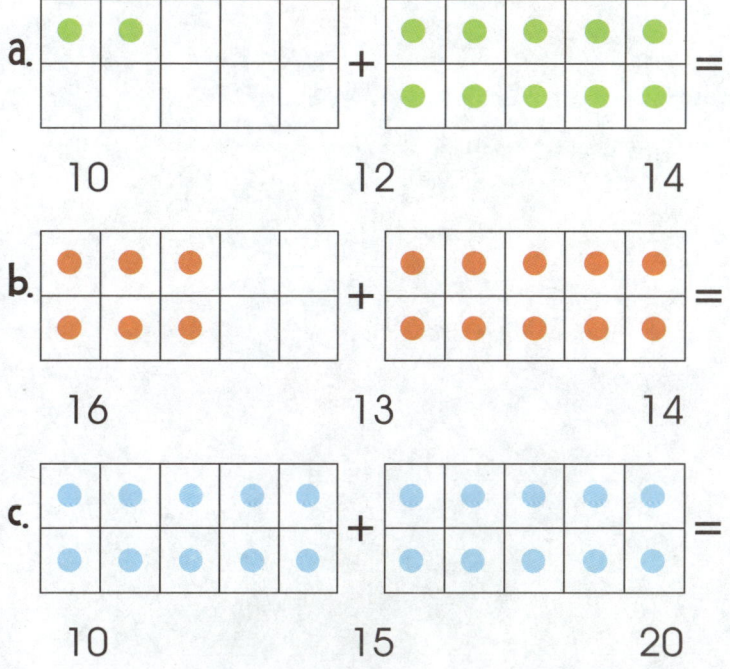

a. [ ] + [ ] =
10   12   14

b. [ ] + [ ] =
16   13   14

c. [ ] + [ ] =
10   15   20

Numbers in Flowers

Add the numbers on the petals and write the answer in the center.

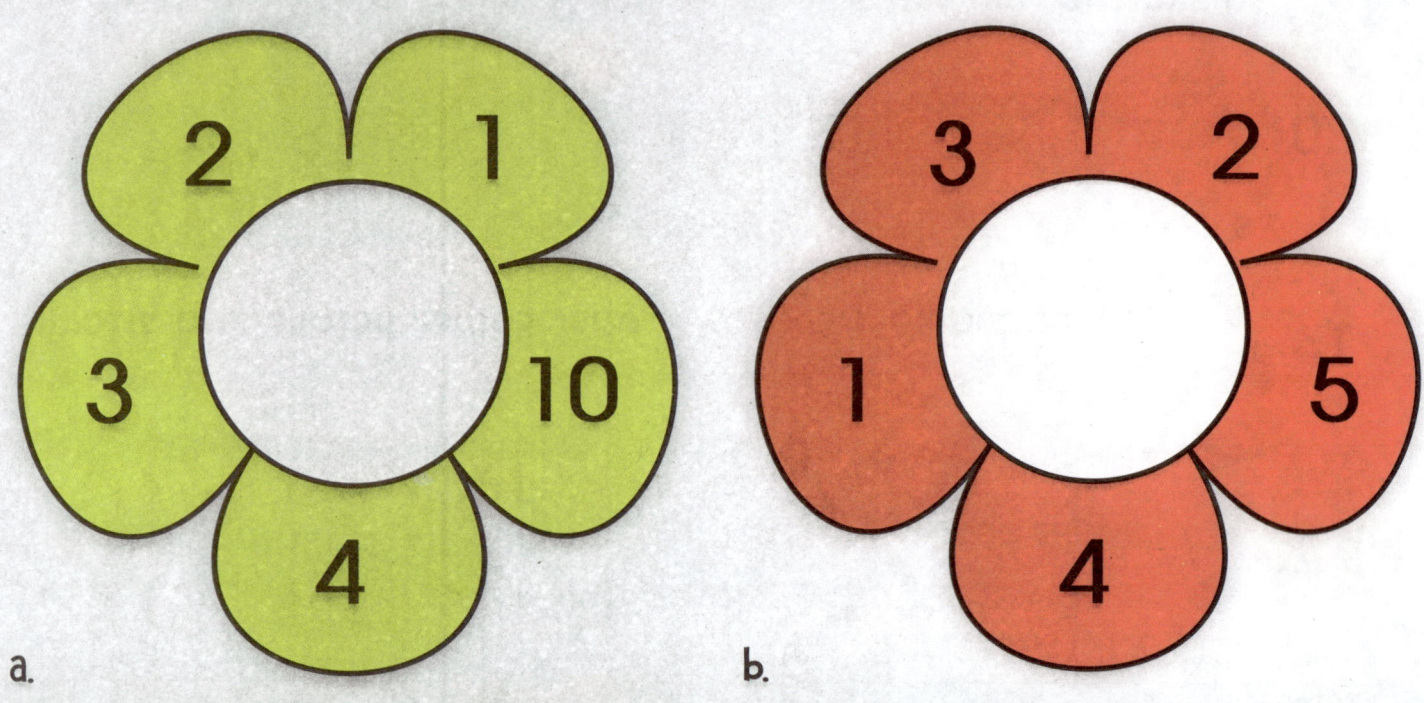

a.

b.

Solve and write.

🌷 =10   🌷 =15   🌷 =6   🌷 =5

a. 🌷 − 🌷 =

b. 🌷 − 🌷 =

c. 🌷 − 🌷 =

d. 🌷 − 🌷 =

Number Bonds

Solve the sums and color the candies of your choice.

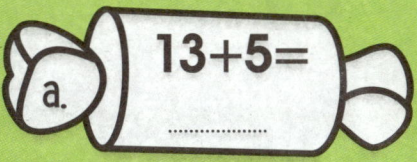

a. 13+5=

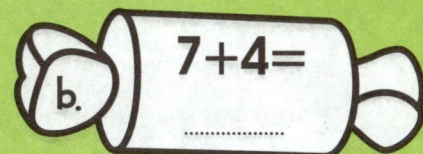

b. 7+4=

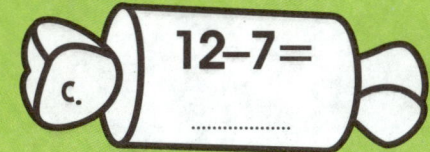

c. 12–7=

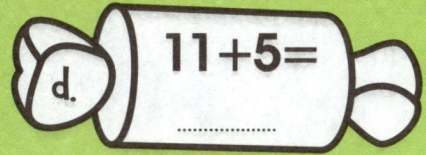

d. 11+5=

e. 15–9=

f. 13+7=

Solve the word problems.

a. 16 bees were putting nectar in a beehive. 3 more bees joined them. How many bees are there now?

b. There were 15 pears on the tree. 11 pear dropped from the pear tree. How many pears are there on the tree now?

c. 12 birds were sitting on a branch. 2 birds flew away. How many birds are there now?

d. 20 eggs were there in the crate. The man dropped 8 eggs by mistake. How many eggs are there in the crate now?

Counting to Fifty

Fill in the missing numbers.

1		3				7	8		10
	12	13	14			17	18		
	22		24		26	27			30
31	32		34	35		37			40
			44	45			48	49	

Count and write the numbers.

a.
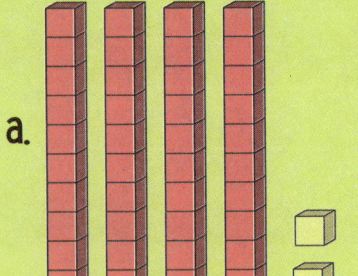

Tens	Ones
4	2

42

b.
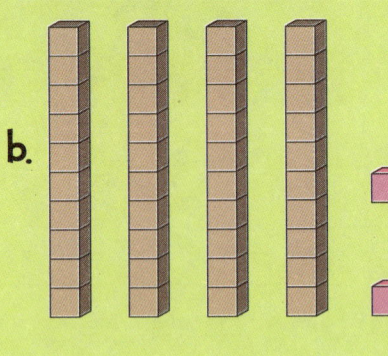

Tens	Ones

c.

Tens	Ones

d.

Tens	Ones

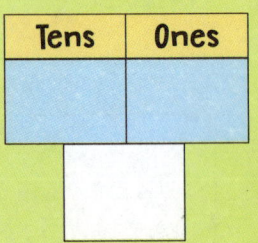

Number Magic

Match the rat with the pumpkin that has the correct answer.

38   a.   47   b.   25   c.   2   d.

1. 16+9   2. 8-6   3. 50-3   4. 31+7

Write the sum of the two numbers on the robot.

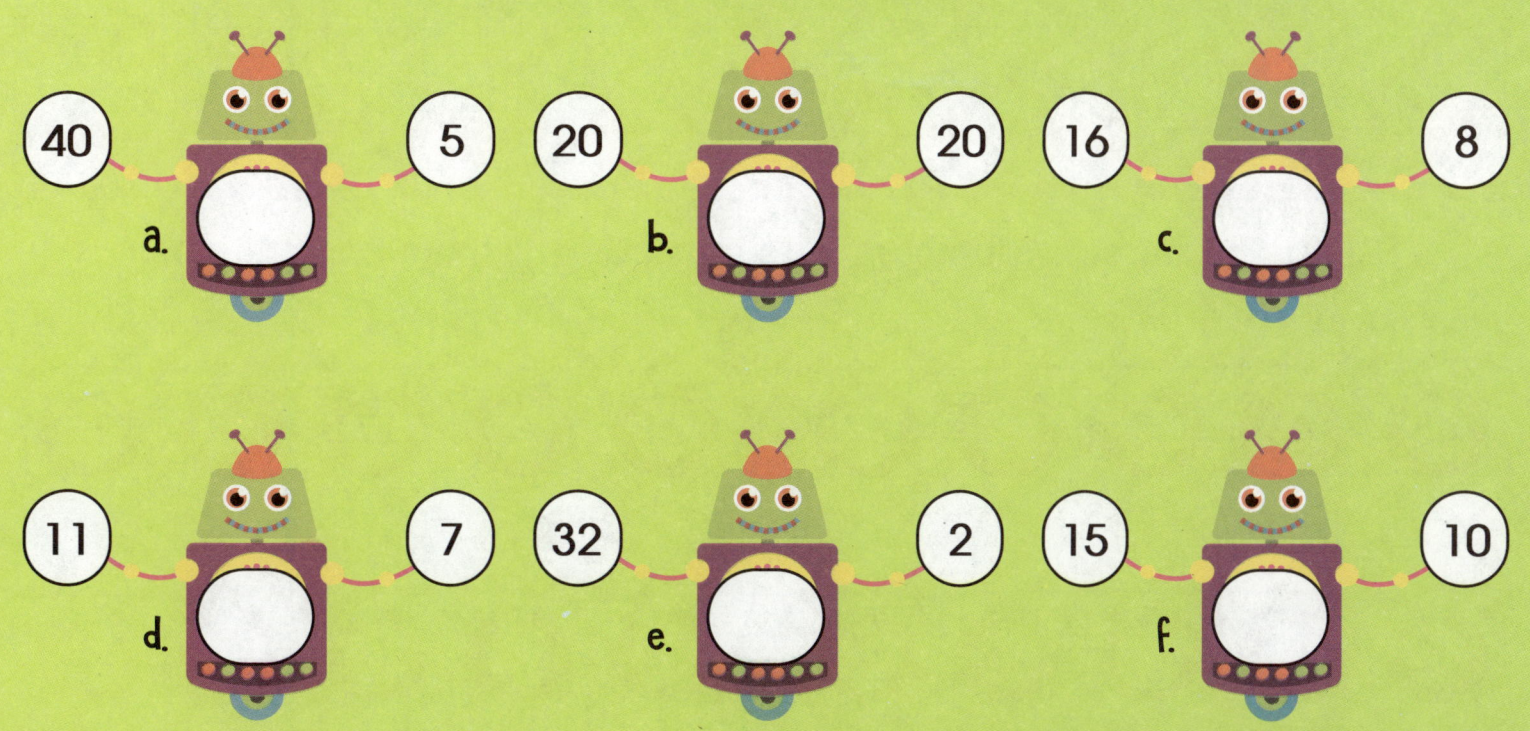

40   5   a.

20   20   b.

16   8   c.

11   7   d.

32   2   e.

15   10   f.

Puzzling Pattern

Which number comes next?

a. 12 16 20 ◯

b. 1 3 5 ◯

c. 9 18 27 ◯

d. 5 10 15 ◯

Identify the pattern and write the missing numbers.

a. 6 12 ___ 24

b. 3 6 9 ___

c. 10 ___ 20 25

d. ___ 14 21 28

FiLL in the missing numbers by subtracting 2 from each tomato.

a. 45 43 ◯ ◯ 37

b. 21 ◯ 17 ◯ 13

c. 32 ◯ ◯ 26 ◯

d. 12 ◯ 8 ◯ 4

Let's Count: Fifty-one to Hundred

Count the coins and write the number.

a.

Tens	Ones
5	3

53

b.

Tens	Ones

c.

Tens	Ones

Count and write the number.

a. ....tens and ....ones

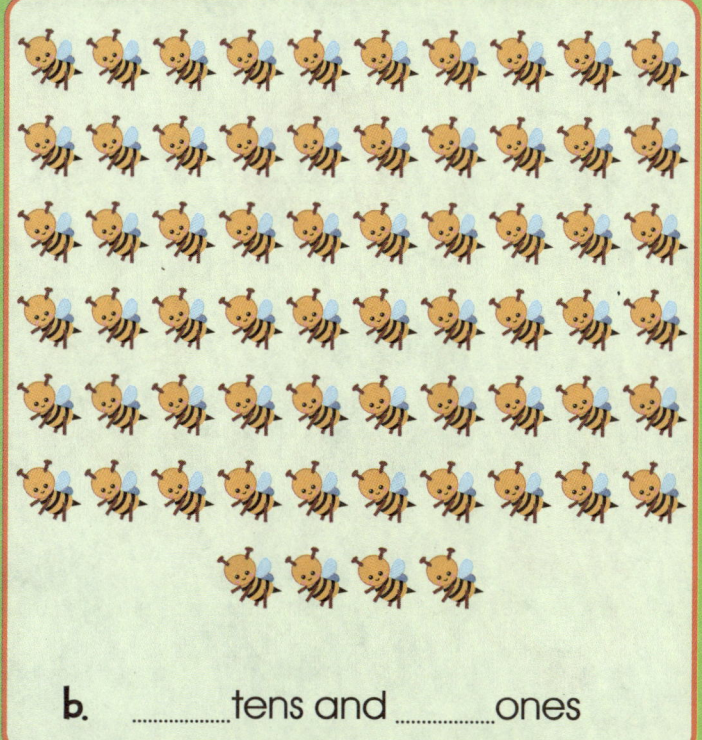

b. ....tens and ....ones

Skip Counting

Skip count by 10s.

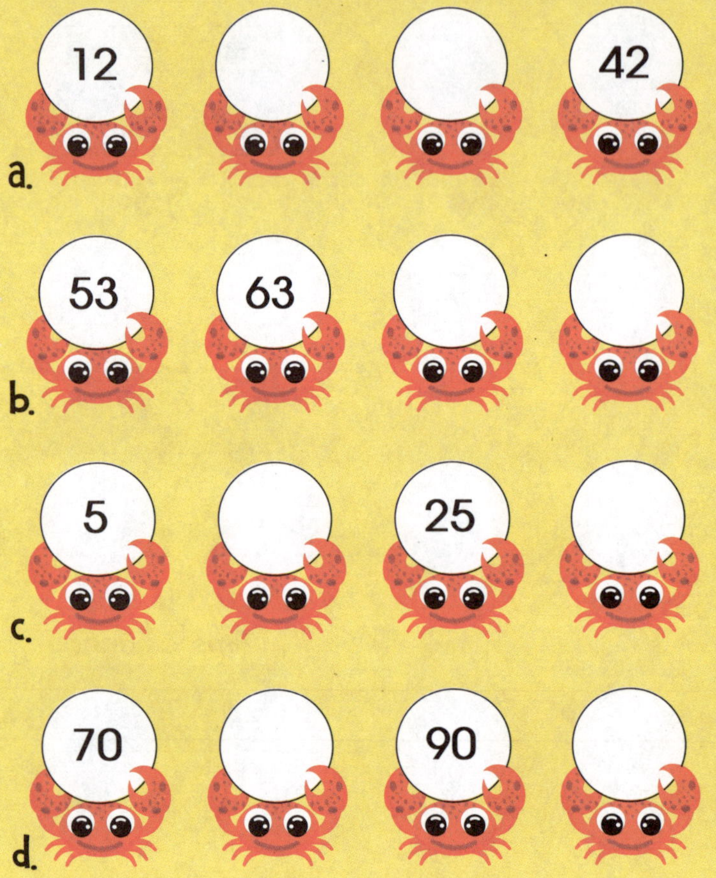

a. 12 | | | 42

b. 53 | 63 | |

c. 5 | | 25 |

d. 70 | | 90 |

Skip count by 5s.

a. 5 | | 15 |

b. 7 | | | 22

c. 64 | 69 | |

d. 58 | | 68 |

Help the first butterfly reach the second butterfly by skipping 2 to each flower.

20 | | |

| | | |

| | | 48

Back Counting

Count back and fill in the missing numbers.

a. 72 __ 70 __ 68 __

b. 15 __ __ __ __ 10

c. 54 __ 52 __ __ 49

d. 20 __ 18 __ __ 15

e. 60 __ __ 57 __ 55

Naming Numbers

Write the number names.

| Ninety | Three | Ten | Fourteen | Seventy-nine |
| Seven | Eleven | Two | Twenty | Six |

a. 90 _____

b. 3 _____

c. 7 _____

d. 10 _____

e. 11 _____

f. 14 _____

g. 2 _____

h. 20 _____

i. 79 _____

j. 6 _____

Match the number names.

a. 1 • • Twenty

b. 100 • • Six

c. 6 • • Five

d. 20 • • Hundred

e. 58 • • One

f. 5 • • Fifty-eight

Match the number names.

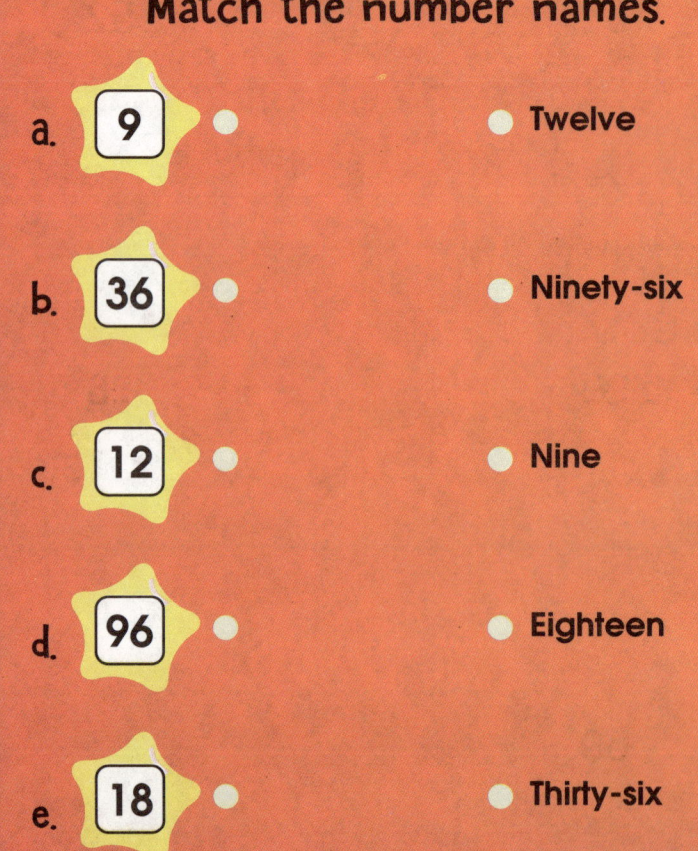

a. 9 • • Twelve

b. 36 • • Ninety-six

c. 12 • • Nine

d. 96 • • Eighteen

e. 18 • • Thirty-six

Ordinal Numbers

A number that indicates the position or order of something in relation to other numbers. Like, first, second, third, and so on.

Ordinal number names.

Color the **First** corn yellow.

Color the **Second** corn orange.

Color the **Third** corn red.

Color the **Fourth** corn pink.

Color the **Fifth** corn purple.

Color the **Sixth** corn green.

Color the **Seventh** corn brown.

Color the **Eighth** corn light blue.

Color the **Ninth** corn light green.

Color the **Tenth** corn gray.

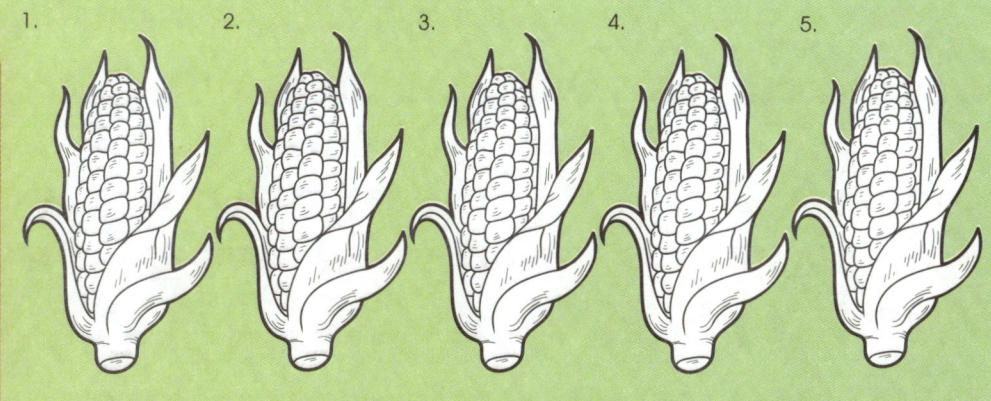

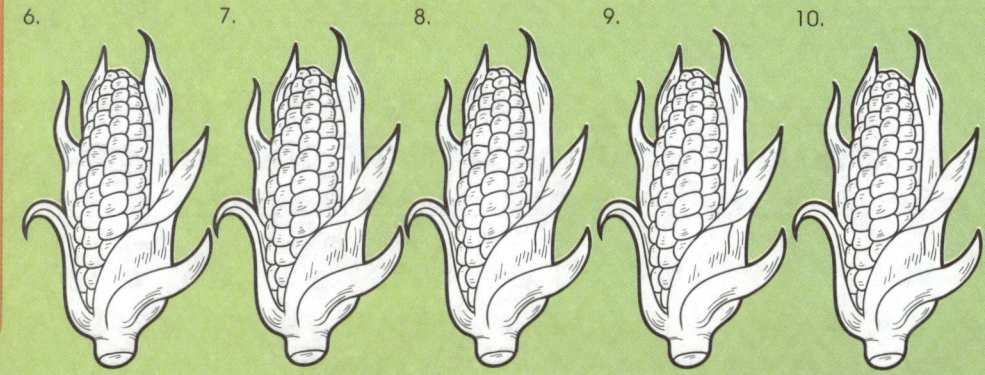

Answer the following questions using ordinal numbers.

Rose

Sunflower

Lily

Daisy

Tulip

Lotus

If the rose is the first flower...

a. Which flower is third?

----

b. Color of the second flower.

----

c. What place is the tulip in?

Color the 5th triangle red and the 1st triangle green.

Even and Odd Numbers

Even numbers are special numbers that can be divided into two equal groups or pairs.

For example, if you have 2 marbles or 6 candies, you can divide them into two groups with 1 marble or 3 candies in each group. This makes them even numbers.

Numbers like 1, 3, 5, or 7 are not even numbers because you can't divide them evenly into two groups with the same number of objects.

Even numbers are those numbers which end with 0,2,4,6,8 and odd numbers are those numbers which end with 1,3,5,7,9.

Count and write the total of odd and even numbers in the space provided.

Odd [ ]   Even [ ]

Color the cupcakes with the even numbers.

a. 32   49   51

b. 19   35   12

Count the number of odd and even candies.

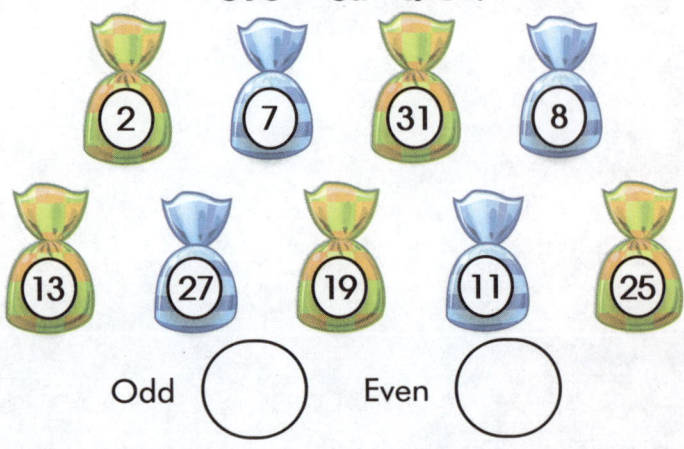

Odd ( )   Even ( )

32

More or Less

Mark the footballs with greater than and less than sign (<,>).

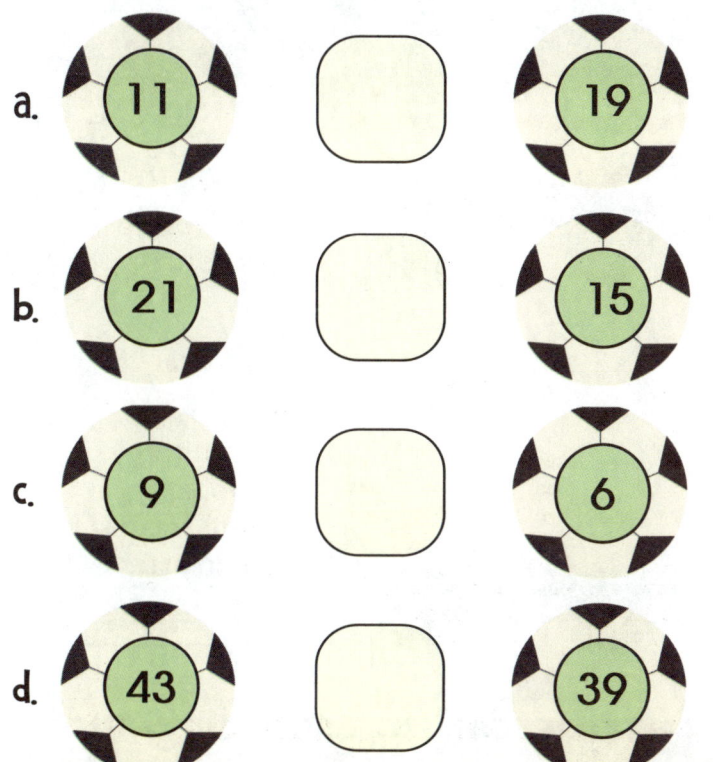

a. 11 ☐ 19

b. 21 ☐ 15

c. 9 ☐ 6

d. 43 ☐ 39

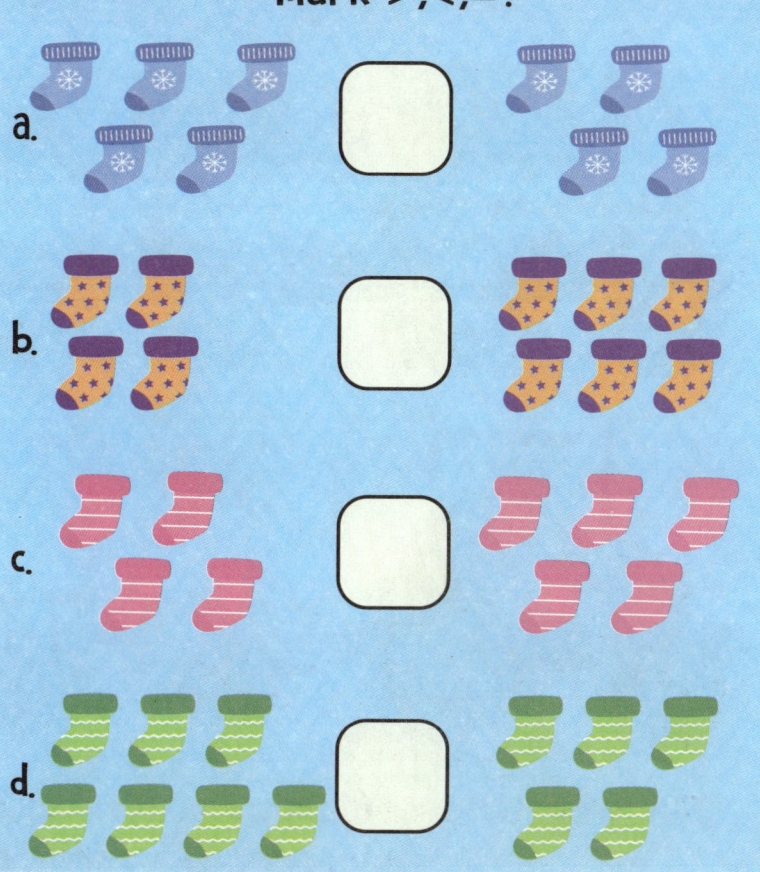

a.

b.

c.

d.

Mark with greater than and less than sign.

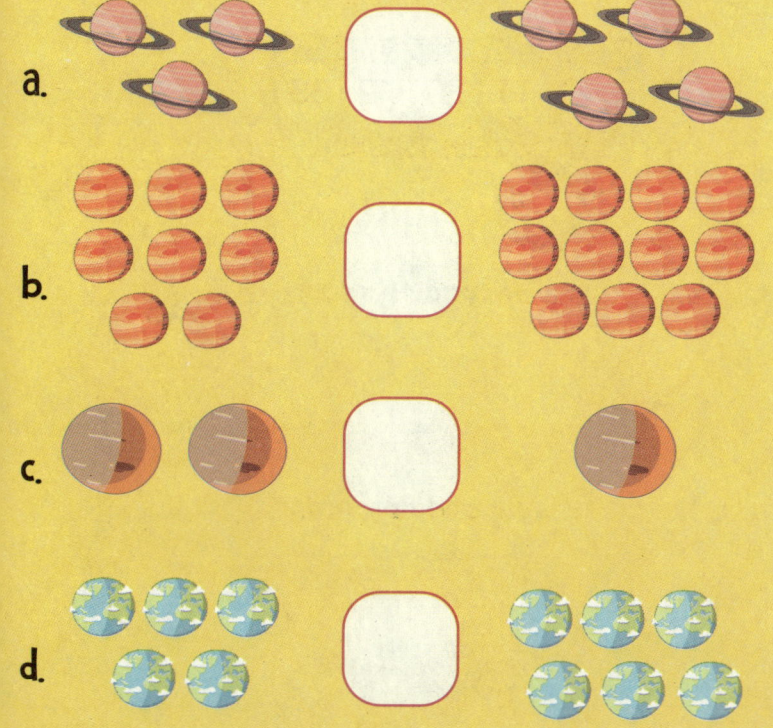

a.

b.

c.

d.

Color the snails—
Greater number with Red color.
Smaller number with Yellow color.

a.  45    98

b.  14    12

c.  11    44

Ascending & Descending

Write the numbers in ascending order.

42 74 3 67

Ascending order. Arranging numbers from smallest to Largest.

Descending order. Arranging numbers from Largest to smallest.

Arrange the numbers written on the pumpkin cart in ascending and descending order on the pumpkin Line.

a. 27 15 45 7 23

b. 4 11 20 42 33

Ascending order

1.

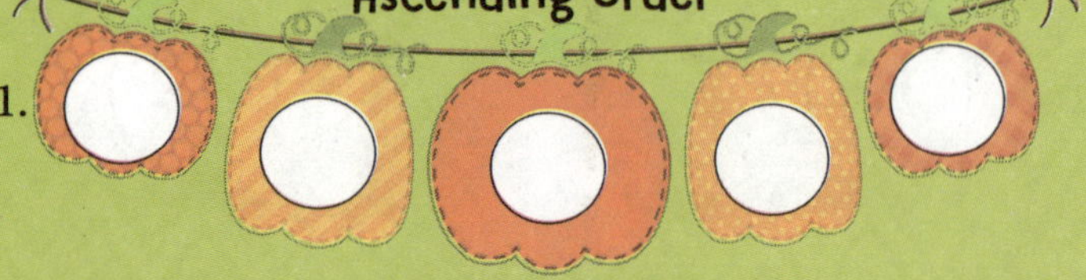

Descending order

2.

Ascending order

1.

Descending order

2.

Number Walls

Fill in the missing numbers on the ice cream scoopes. The numbers at the bottom add up to the number on top.

a. 7
2 + 5

b.
8 4

c. 9
7

d. 6
1

e.
2 3

The number on each cookie is equal to the sum of two cookies below it. Fill the boxes with the correct number on the cookie pyramid.

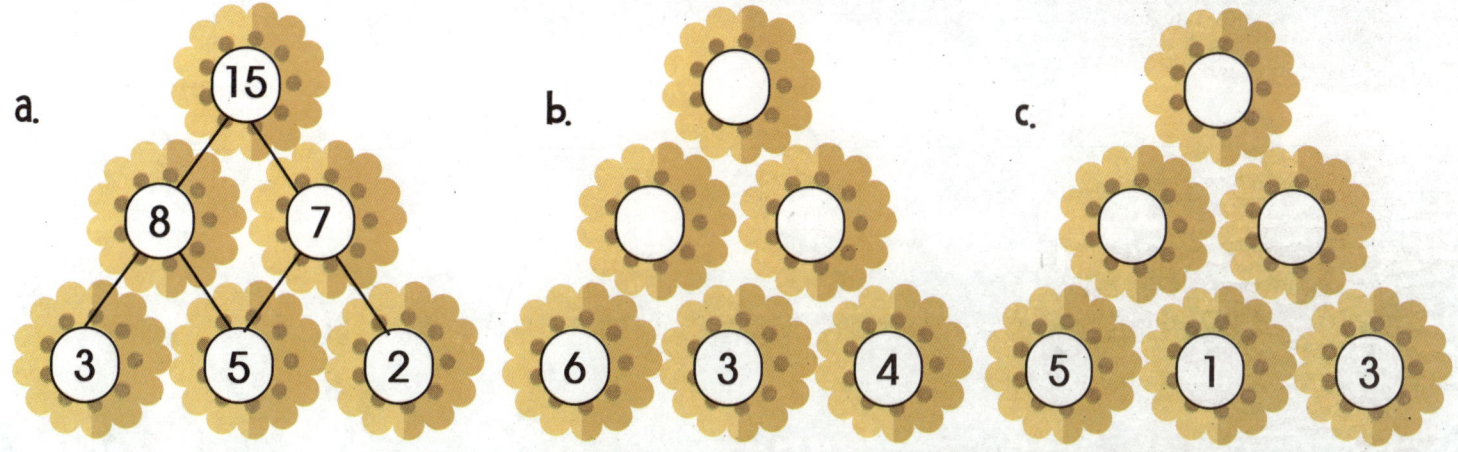

a. 15
8 7
3 5 2

b.
6 3 4

c.
5 1 3

Solve the Christmas pyramid. The number on each ball is equal to the sum of two balls below it.

a.
13
4 9 6

b.
11 22 9

c.
17 12 16

d.
14 16 39

Decoding Numbers

Count and write the number of each fruit in the jar and then solve the sums.

🍎 ☐   🟣 ☐   🟢 ☐   🍐 ☐

a. 🍎 + 🍐 + 🟢 = ☐

b. 🟣 + 🍎 + 🟣 = ☐

c. 🟢 + 🍐 + 🍐 = ☐

d. 🍎 + 🟢 + 🟢 = ☐

e. 🟣 + 🟣 + 🍎 = ☐

Count and write the value, then solve the sums.

🦀 ☐   🪼 ☐   🐟 ☐

a. 🦀 🦀 + 🐟 🐟 = ☐

b. 🪼 + 🦀 🦀 = ☐

c. 🐟 🐟 + 🪼 🪼 = ☐

Solve each problem and write the matching letter on the blank above the answer.

A	9−3	N	6+5	M	8+5	T	9−4	U	6+4
Y	4+5	O	7−3	B	9−2	C	8+7	H	9+9
S	6+8	E	7+9						

Why do bees have sticky hair?

```
----  ----  ----  ----  ----  ----  ----        ----  ----  ----  ----
 7    16    15     6    10    14    16            5    18    16     9
```

```
----  ----  ----     ----  ----  ----  ----  ----     ----  ----  ----  ----  ----
10    14    16       18     4    11    16     9       15     4    13     7    14
```

Solve the picture code puzzle and write the number in the given space.

 10    2    4    5

a. 🏠 + 🥣🥣 + 🔴 = ⬜

b. 🖌🖌🖌 🔴 − 🥣 + 🖌 = ⬜

c. 🔴🥣 + 🖌🖌 − 🔴 = ⬜

d. 🔴🔴🔴🔴 + 🖌 + 🥣 = ⬜

Tricky Puzzles

Draw each bee's route to the purple flower, following the instructions.

Go across the maze by solving the sums and
following number 5.

2+2	1+4	4+1	2+3	5+0	←		
3+1	5+0	2+4	5+6	5+4	4+2	2+4	1+3
4+2	3+2	5+1	5+4	6+2	7+2	2+6	1+7
3+3	4+1	1+4	3+6	7+2	2+2	1+3	7+5
5+6	5+4	5+0	2+3	3+2	→		

Brain Benders

Write five more, five Less than the number given in the box.

five more +5					
a.	66	34	18	93	22
five Less -5					

five more +5					
b.	88	67	10	74	33
five Less -5					

Add the number written in the center with the middle ring number.

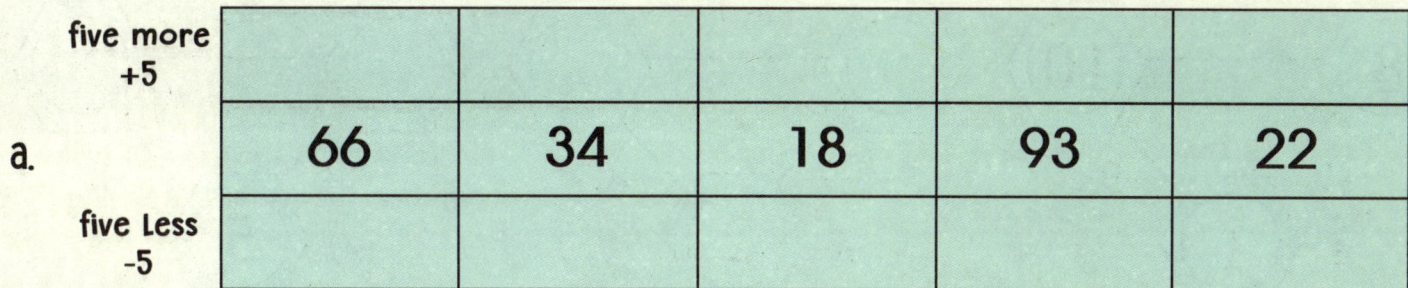

a.
19
8 13
3 **6** 5
15 10
3 16

b.
3 13
5 **15** 25
22 20
11 13

c.
8 12
3 **21** 4
14 16
23 6

d.
19
8 13
3 **6** 5
15 10
3 16

e.
3 13
5 **15** 25
22 20
11 13

f.
8 12
3 **21** 4
14 16
23 6

39

Fun with a Twist

Solve the following sums.

a.
8 — +2 — 10
+7   -9
1

b.
○ — +1 — ○
+7   -8
2

c.
○ — +2 — ○
-4   +2
5

d.
1 — +3 — ○
+6   -2
○

e.
○ — +2 — ○
+5   -7
9

f.
○ — +2 — ○
+4   -6
4

g.
○ — +1 — ○
+3   -4
6

h.
○ — -6 — ○
+4   +2
4

i.
○ — +4 — ○
-8   +4
9

j.
○ — +9 — ○
-2   -7
3

Let's Revise

Solve the sums and color according to the instructions.

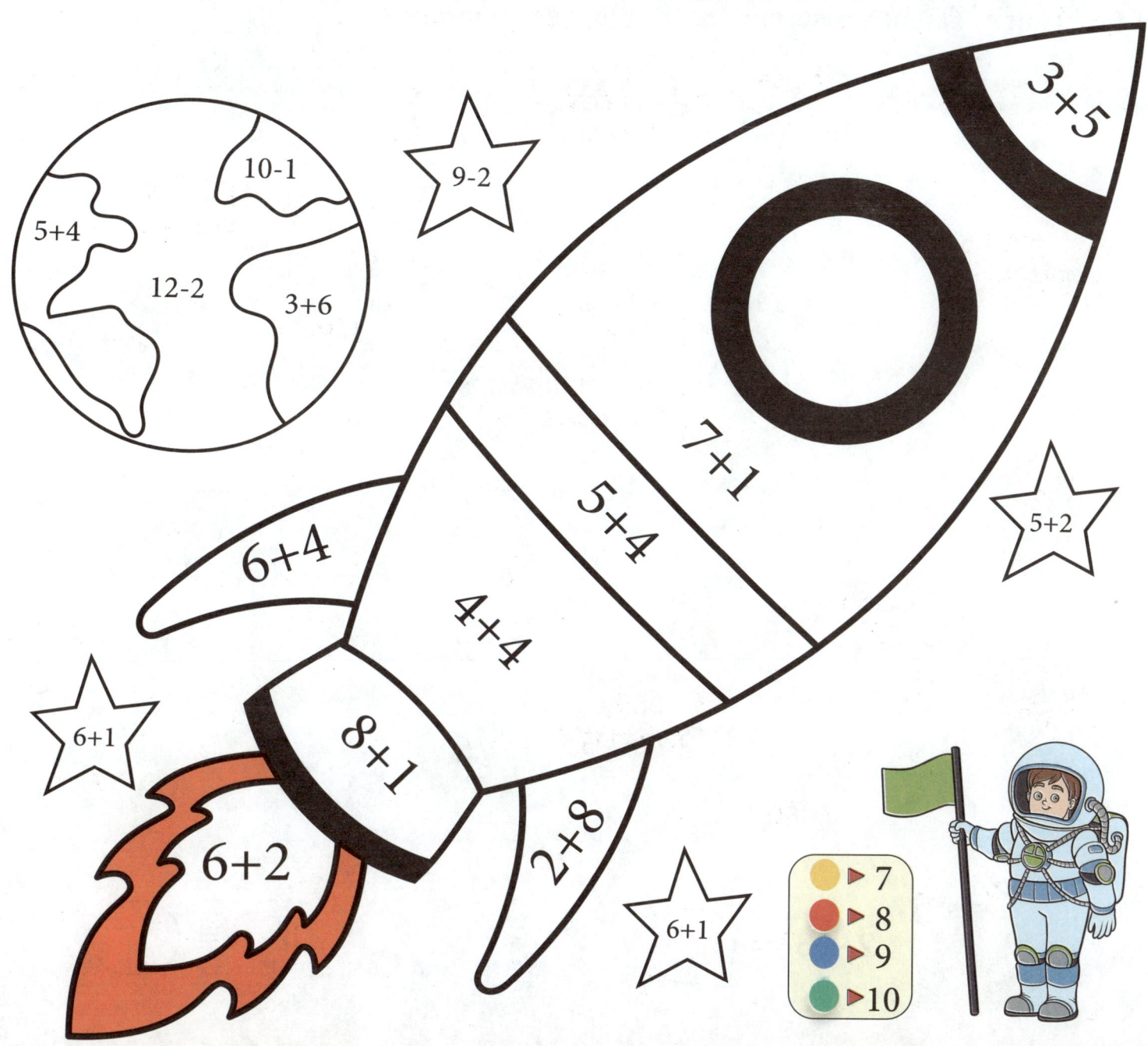

Tick the correct answer.

a. ⬤⬤⬤ - ⬤⬤ = 4 / 1

b. 🌙🌙🌙🌙 + 🌙🌙🌙 = 7 / 2

c. 🧑‍🚀🧑‍🚀🧑‍🚀🧑‍🚀 - 🧑‍🚀🧑‍🚀 = 2 / 6

Follow the instructions given in the bubbles and see where the animals land. Then fill the answers in the spaces given below.

1

2 — I hop forward 8

3

4

I fly back 4

15

14

13

I Crawl back 5

16

5

20 — I fly back 5

12

I add 2

11

19

18

17

6

I fly forward 6

10

9

8

7

a. 2 + 8 = ◯

b. 13 − 4 = ◯

c. 16 − 5 = ◯

d. 20 − 5 = ◯

e. 11 + 2 = ◯

f. 10 + 6 = ◯

Solve and write.

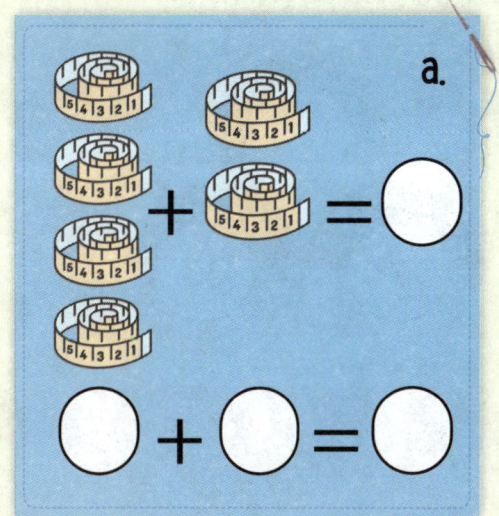

a.

$$\bigcirc + \bigcirc = \bigcirc$$

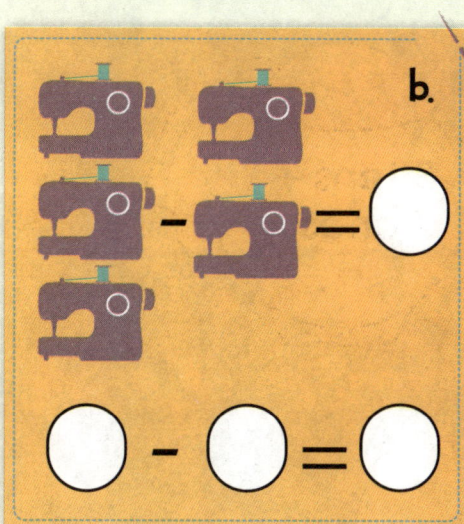

b.

$$\bigcirc - \bigcirc = \bigcirc$$

c.

$$\bigcirc + \bigcirc = \bigcirc$$

Write the missing numbers.

a.

42, ___, 38, ___

b.

64, ___, ___, 67

c.

78, 83, ___, ___

Color by number.

- 🟡 2+2
- 🟤 7-5
- 🟠 4-3
- 🟢 6-3

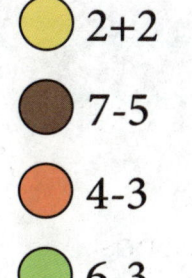

43

Write the number on the Label.

a. 5 tens + 3 ones =

b. 3 tens + 7 ones =

c. 1 tens + 0 ones =

d. 7 tens + 5 ones =

e. 8 tens + 2 ones =

Add the numbers in the ice cream pyramid.

a. 7   33

_____ tens and _____ ones

b. 6   61

_____ tens and _____ ones

Count the tens and ones, then write the number.

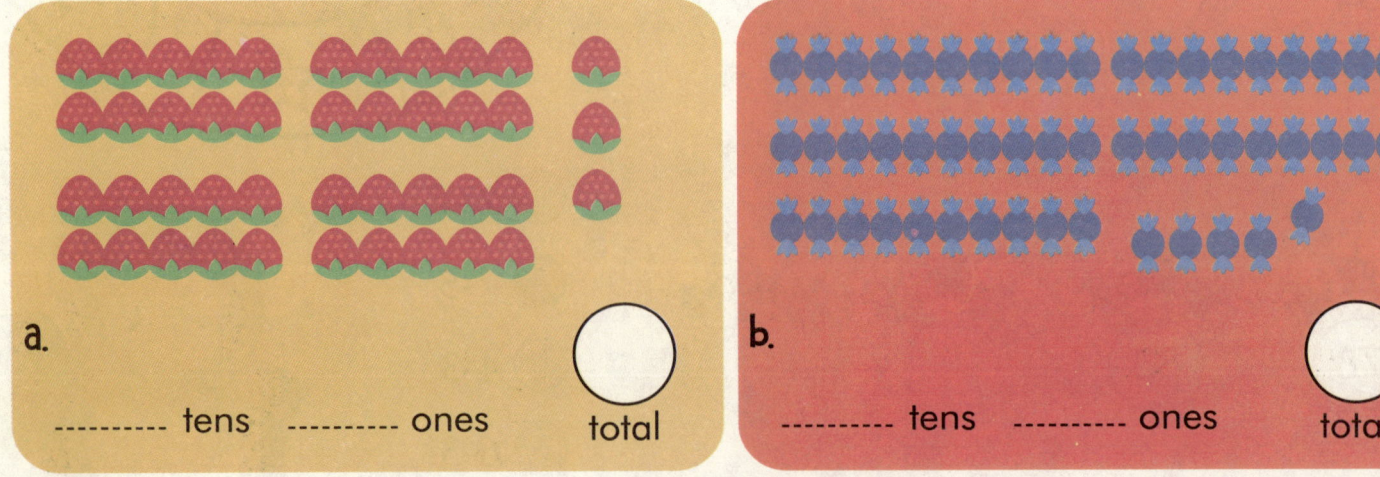

a. _____ tens _____ ones   total

b. _____ tens _____ ones   total

Write 2 numbers before and after the given number.

Before   After

a. 82

b. 14

c. 61

d. 33

a. Eric bought 5 snacks at the fun carnival. He later bought 3 more. How many snacks in total does he have?

b. There are 15 apples in a basket. Mason ate 3 apples. How many apples remain in the basket?

c. There are 9 potatoes on a table. Rio picks up 2. How many potatoes are left on the table?

d. Jane bought 6 balloons and her friend Macy bought 8 balloons at the carnival. How many balloons did they buy in total?

Fill in the number wheel. Add the number in the center with the numbers in the middle ring.

a.

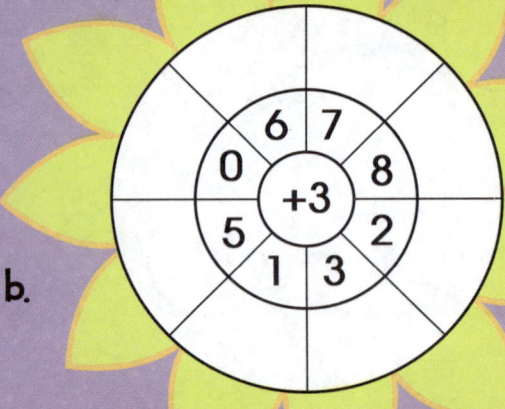

b.

c.

d.

Even numbers in outer ring   --

Odd numbers in outer ring   --

Color the even numbers red and odd numbers green.

Answers

Page 2

1. 2,3,4,6,7,8,9
2. a. 2,4, b. 6,8,
c. 5,6, d. 5,8

Page 3

1. a. 3, b. 4,
c. 1, d. 2
2. a. 7, b. 4, c. 2

Page 4

1. a. 8, b. 6, c. 9,
e. 6

Page 6

a. 8,
b. 7,
c. 5

Page 7

a. 9,
b. 9,
c. 4,
d. 6

Page 8

1. a. 5, b. 9, c. 4
2. b. $3+1=4$,
c. $5+4=9$

Page 9

a. 8,
b. 5,
c. 8,
d. 3,
e. 7,
f. 8

Page 10

1. a. 6,
b. 3,
c. 1,
d. 5

Page 11

a. 6,
b. 2,
c. 1,
d. 3

Page 12

1. a. 5,
b. 2,
c. 2
2. a. 1, b. 2,
c. 3, d. 4

Page 13

a. 2,
b. 1,
c. 4,
d. 4,
e. 1,
f. 7

Page 14

b. 6,
c. 9,
d. 8

Page 15

1. a. 7,
b. 9,
c. 8,
d. 9
2. a. 2,
b. 5

Page 16

a. 11,
b. 16,
c. 14

Page 18

1. a. 13, b. 14,16,
c. 20
3. a. 9, b. 8, c. 10
4. a. 19, b. 17, c.16

Page 19

1. a. 10, b. 13,
c. 4, d. 1
2. a. 11, b. 6,
c. 8, d. 20
3. a.11, b. 19, c. 5
4. a. 14,16, b. 18,20,
c. 8,10

Page 20

a. 1 tens 3 ones,
b. 1 tens 4 ones,
c. 1 tens 4 ones,
d. 1 tens 6 ones,

Page 21

1. a. 2 tens 0 ones,
b. 1 tens 4 ones,
c. 1 tens 2 ones,
d. 1 tens 8 ones
2. a. 16, b. 19,
c. 10, d. 20
4. a. 12, b. 14, c. 20

Page 22

1. a. 20, b. 15
2. a. 5, b. 9,
c. 5, d. 1

Page 23

1. a. 17, b. 11, c. 5,
d. 16, e. 6, f. 20
2. a. 19, b. 4,
c. 10, d. 12

Page 24

b. 4 tens 4 ones,
c. 3 tens 1 ones,
d. 3 tens 0 ones,

Page 25

1. a. 4, b. 3,
c.1, d. 2
2.a. 45, b.40, c. 24,
d. 18, e. 34, f. 25

Page 26

1. a. 24, b. 7,
c. 36, d. 20
2. a. 18, b. 12,
c. 15, d. 7
3. a. 41,39, b. 19,15,
c. 30,28,24, d. 10,6

Page 27

1. b. 6 tens 5 ones,
c. 7 tens 7 ones,
2. a. 5 tens 6 ones,
b. 6 tens 4 ones,

Page 28

1. a. 22,32, b. 73,83,
c. 15,35, d. 80,100
2. a. 10,25, b. 12,17,
c. 74,79, d. 63,73
3. 22,24,26,28,30,32,
34,36,38,40,42,44,46

Page 29

a. 71,69,67
b. 14,13,12,11
c. 53,51,50
d. 19,17,16
e. 59,58,56

Page 30

1. a. ninety, b. three, c. seven, d. ten, e. eleven,
f. fourteen, g. twenty, i. seventy-nine, j. six
2. a. one, b. hundred, c. six, d. twenty,
e. fifty-eight, f. five
3. a. nine, b. thirty-six, c. twelve, d. ninety-six,
e. eighteen

Page 31-32

a. Lily, b. Yellow,
c. Fifth

---

1. Odd-2, Even-4
3. Odd-7, Even-2

Page 33

1. a. 11<19,
b. 21>15, c. 9>6,
d. 43>39
2. a. >, b. <,
c. <, d. >
3. a. <, b. <,
c. >, d. <

Page 34

1. 3,42,67,74
a. 1. 7,15,23,27,45
2. 45,27,23,15,7
b. 1. 4,11,20,33,42
2. 42,33,20,11,4

Page 35

1. b. 12,c. 2, d. 5, e. 5
2. b. 16,9,7
c. 10,6,4
3. a. 15, b. 33,31,
c. 29,28, d. 30,55

Page 36

1. 2,5,5,4
a. 11, b. 12,
c. 13, d. 12
2. 6,4,6
a. 12+12=24
b. 4+12=16
c. 12+8=20

Page 37

1. BEACAUSE THEY
USE HONEY COMB
2. a. 22, b. 15,
c. 13, d. 26

Page 39

1. a. 71,39,23,98,27
b. 61,29,13,88,17
2. a. 93,72,15,79,38
b. 83,62,5,69,28

Page 40

b. 9,10, c. 1,3,
d. 0, e. 14,16 f. 8,10,
g. 9,10, h. 8,2,
i. 1,5, j. 1,10

Page 42

a. 10, b. 9, c. 11,
d. 15, e. 13, f. 16

Page 43

1. a. 4+2=6,
b. 3-2=1, c. 4+1=5
2. a. 40,36, b. 65,66,
c. 88,93

Page 44

1. a. 53, b. 37, c. 10,
d. 75, e. 82
2. a. 40- 4 tens 0 ones,
b. 67- 6 tens 7 ones
3. a. 4 tens 3 ones=43
b. 5 tens 5 ones=55

Page 45

1. a. Before-78,80
After- 84,86,
b. Before-10,12
After- 16,18
c. Before-57,59
After- 63,65
d. Before-29,31
After- 35,37
2. a. 8 snacks,
b. 12 apples, c. 7 potatoes,
d. 14 balloons